The Sound of the Earth Singing to Herself

Ricky Ray

First published October 2020 by Fly on the Wall Press

Published in the UK by

Fly on the Wall Press

56 High Lea Rd

New Mills

Derbyshire

SK22 3DP

www.flyonthewallpoetry.co.uk

ISBN: 978-1-913211-31-8

Copyright Ricky Ray © 2020

Supported using public funding by

**ARTS COUNCIL
ENGLAND**

LOTTERY FUNDED

for Addie, Bonnie and Safora

Acknowledgments

Wholehearted thanks to the editors of the following publications for giving many of these poems their first moments in the light: *The American Scholar; Forklift, Ohio; Deaf Poets Society; Friends of the Mississippi River; Iamb; Diode Poetry Journal and Sporklet.*

Endless love to everyone who helped the work find its way up: Isabelle Kenyon, for believing in this book and being a dream to work with; my mentors at Bennington, for teaching an old dog new tricks: Jenny Boully, April Bernard, Carmen Gimenez Smith, Craig Morgan Teicher and Mark Wunderlich; my workshop fam, for pushing me past my natural resting places; my journal editors, for teaching me when the work is ready: David Lehman, Matt Hart, Sarah Katz, Leslie Thomas, Mark Antony Owen, Patty Paine and Dorothy Chan; my blurb ninjas, for dropping my jaw with your yin and yang: Dylan Krieger and Devin Kelly; Christoffer Relander and Christian Ericson, for the exquisiteness of the cover; my doggy and kitty loves, my deepest family, for guiding me, guarding me and teaching me the art of living: Rascal, Addie, Bonnie, Bailey and Charlie—for you, I wish these poems were full of duck hearts, fish juice and butter; mama Earth, for the line of verse that is my brief turn in your song; and Safora, my wife and my life—as ever, the best of me comes from what happens when I'm with you.

Praise for
'The Sound of the Earth Singing to Herself'

"Ricky Ray's *The Sound of the Earth Singing to Herself* is a private archive of "unholstered" embodiment, imagining disability not as a disconnect or alienation from the environment but as a curious kinship with it, a shared "scream" in which there is no difference between "agony" and "ecstasy," the speaker's body and "Oklahoma," "generations of teeth" and "somewhere in Indiana." This is a new song of an old but still echoing America, in which "sludgehearted" monsters emerge triumphant while families live on "dog biscuits," frantically attempting to preserve whatever is "left of a god." Both cruelly and comfortingly, *Earth Singing* reminds us every god and monster in this country, including the land, will "go to rot" together one day. And whether characterized as tragic or sublime, this coalescence is a melody we are already humming deep down."

—Dylan Krieger, author of *Giving Godhead* (Delete, 2017), *The Mother Wart* (Vegetarian Alcoholic, 2019), *Metamortuary* (Nine Mile, 2020) and *Soft-Focus Slaughterhouse* (11:11, forthcoming).

"In one of the poems in this chapbook, Ricky Ray writes "living takes time, and I want you / to stay with me." It's just one tender, honest moment in this collection of deep, effervescent tenderness. Throughout *The Sound of the Earth Singing to Herself*, Ricky's poems ask the world to stay just a little longer. They admit, with grace, what they don't understand. They offer thanks. But what they do most singularly is care. Ricky's poems care about life, love, dogs, birds, gentleness, unknowing, wonder, and more. Poetry is a kind of witness, and each poem in this chapbook bears such gentle witness to this world, a world that sings and kills and births, all at once. They, as one poem states, "sneak a peak" even when the world's "too tender" to watch. What to do when the world is not enough? Read Ricky's poems. What to do when the yearning feels unbearable? Read Ricky's poems. What to do when you want to heal, even when healing feels impossible? Read Ricky's poems. To read this book is to learn, just a little bit better, how to live."

—Devin Kelly, author of *In This Quiet Church of Night, I Say Amen* **(Civil Coping Mechanisms, 2017) and** *Blood on Blood* **(Unknown Press, 2016)**

Contents

Prelude: Quiet Opens the Door

It's snowing,
and the mind is most beautiful
when she whispers
her thoughts

so far down
into quiet,

one can hear an idea
echo all the way back to creation,

and the Universe—that quivering mouse—
has a chance to slip out
into the owl-less hours
to admire what's become of itself.

Sometimes Vision Withers on the Vine

Electricity was a luxury in that clapboard house—
three rooms and ten thousand fleas—

flowed as scarce as running water
because crack was more alluring than the bills.

25¢ mac and cheese, every night for years,
a burn the size of a thumb on the dull-red plastic bowl.

Hand-me-downs, barefoot in ditches, my finger
tracing the edges of ringworm's beautiful bruise.

For baths, we ran a hose from the neighbor's faucet,
and through the window, by the dim light of the lamp,

I watched Mrs. Morrissey take off her bra.
Once, three hits into the pipe,

my father's friend set candle after candle
in the center of his palm,

lit it and stared until the flame went out,
wax spilling through his fingers onto the floor.

I sometimes wonder what he saw
in that dance of light, and sometimes,

I don't have to wonder—
I see it, too:

the shiny forehead, the hollow eyes,
my mother's chin, my father's jaw,

my lips moving soundlessly
while the ghost of the ghost

of the living body makes his rounds,
peering into each version of my future,

where nothing happens,
and the only thing left to do

is turn out the light.

The End of My Brother

He couldn't walk, eat, and my father didn't tell me
until after he put my brother to sleep—
a kindness I never wanted, still don't: *take it back.*

There was a hole the size of a pawprint in my chest
so I went outside to give my eyes something to do.
I remember it was hard to cry, as though the news

had blown out all moisture and made of my body
Oklahoma. There was something about the sky,
the way it bled, dimming over the horizon

where my brother went to bark and never came back.
Pass me a beer, I said to someone who wasn't there,
I just want to hold it till all the cold is gone,

and I wasn't talking about the can. Too warm,
we call it, when the inner and outer match.
Imagine Florida and two inches of fur.

Imagine a dog who saved my father from alcohol
and despair. He was my brother, my guardian,
my teacher, my guide, and he raised me

on a savage hunger for every morsel of this world:
we drooled *fuck yes* at the dog biscuits,
the only food left in the house. So dry, so dry:

maybe *that's* what my grief recalled.
I used to throw my head back and bark when
I was young. (Rascal and I had long late talks.)

When I was fourteen, we lived alone together
for nine months, the animal just one of seven kingdoms
we inhaled. When he was fourteen, he sniffed the woman

who put the needle in his neck. (I wasn't there, I wasn't there.)
I've yipped a bit but haven't howled at the moon since.
The low rumble of a growl, however, has never left

the spitworn nest of emptiness in my throat.

A Thimbleful of Blood

Every day at five-fifteen I drink a pint of tea,
one hundred and seventy degrees—Snow Dragon—
the subtlest scent, the tea's character
so close to water, the barest tip of a leaf
announcing the end of the beast's hibernation.
More than a pint is greed. Less is a lack of passion.
With each sip, a little fire on the tongue,
the dragon comes to life.

And when he lifts his head from under his wing,
when the opening of his eyes awakens everything
in the valley, and the rivers swell and swiften,
and two children, playing games,
try to push each other in, watch out.

And when we, in our creaturely cohabitation,
make a game of out-maneuvering one another,
when we eye the mouth of extinction
as it closes in on us, and elbow our way
into the flock, kicking our kin that they might
slow down, thinking *him and not me,* watch out.

What's Left

I set desire / on fire / and she screamed
I couldn't tell / if the scream
was agony / or ecstasy

what's the difference?

my back / probably wants / to stop hurting
but having killed / for years
and years / without relief

just one moment of comfort

and by comfort I mean / pain
that relents / from a knife-twist
to a dog gnawing / an old / old bone

just one primal grunt of ache unshouldered

blood unholstered / and I swear
there would be / nothing better
than bending over

to pick up what's left of my life.

(Dis)ability

Some days, my body is so beautiful
I can't believe I get to live here.

Toward What

To walk down the flaking
concrete steps, watch a mother
shift child from hip to hip
and sigh the way an old master
commands canvas to take on

vision, vermilion, the eventualities
of breastmilk—to place my hand
on the small of my back and dig,
as if I could claw out the pain
and throw it away—to sniff the air

and wonder which walk to take
(because walking has come
into these legs again)—
to ask Addie to go slowly
while I limp to the corner and back—

to fall once and take three
minutes to ascend six stairs
is quite enough test
of endurance to call this
a triumphant day.

The Dance

I turn up my collar and Addie the scent-sleuth
walks me between the invisible signposts of smell.
The air's crisp, moist with the promise of snow.
What do fire hydrants and bushes have in common?
Good places to pee. She watches my hand
for the ritual dip towards the pocket of treats.
I watch her sly weaving, the way she'll huddle
over a bone, as if merely sniffing the news.

I've become an authority on her calculations.
And she an authority on how to play me.
Good girl. Yes, eventually, the entire pocketful
is for you. You know it and I know you know it
and I know you want it all right now.
But living takes time, and I want you
to stay with me, out of the vet's hands,
the bone sharp as an arrow in your throat.

One overlong sniff and I know to bend quick,
hand ready to snatch from her mouth,
but this time she's still, her head cocked,
ears perked, so I ask: *what is it, girlie?*
Under the bushes: a couple of bites' worth
of sparrow. Brown and white shrieking,
she pecks at the head and chest of her mate: flat,
tucked in his suit, quiet as wood on the mulch.

She seems manic, flawless, circling his head,
her steps shaping in the soil a halo. She pecks and pulls,
pecks and pulls, as if to stand her lover back up.
Normally, a storm blows through and the nestlings fall
and break their necks. Normally, Addie discovers
the dead and we pick up and carry, find places to bury
the bodies we find on our walks. She discovers
the survivors, too—more than a few owe her their lives.

But today, we leave the widow to fight for her mate.
He looks so calm, absorbing her grief into him
where it will leave her alone—the last thing she wants.
Tomorrow, it will snow. And the day after: snow.
And the day after, the snow will thaw, when Addie and I
again will come walking, sniffing to find all of them
gone: the body, the soul, the fresh scent of grief,
and the widow, so near to death she stared at its jaws
and danced, three inches from the mouth of a dog.

The Dream

In which the monster emerged sludgehearted and fond of hares.
And triplets were born of a wish that blew itself apart.
Candleflame ignored the wind.

                                        Her face, thirty years on ice,
the one my waking mind can't find in the crowd.
Water in the streets so high you could swim.

                                                I was a woman.
I was a wolf. I could hear hunger as a longing for death,
blood as one continuous song. My toes wriggled
as scrollwork along dark's
invisible score.

                              What comes now, in the quietest
hour, under the skin, the senses so flammable they ignite
at the slightest…

                                  a house loses its dreamers, an owl dives,
blood forgets the curses it casts like crows over the moors.

Somewhere in Indiana

About twenty klicks east of the Mississippi, rain fills a bucket with hope, but the bucket leaks, has been sitting so long with its rust whispering henna to dirt, the black dirt, that the farm it once belonged to has faded from memory, as have the forms of value that lead from seed to mouth, where generations of teeth crumble and fall out, where kids develop poorly not for lack of something to eat but for lack of nutrients in their food, and the land that used to be a farm that used to be a cougar's valley has changed hands many times, it has passed between people that never once dug their fingers into the Earth's body, never once felt her cool shiver as they brought her black soul I mean soil into the light, never carried her with them indoors, never spent five minutes digging her out from under their nails, they've never known this pleasure, they call it labor and shudder at the thought, like a filthy deed, like a punishment to be avoided, oblivious to the dullness in their eyes and their speech, where the names for things have receded into words like bird and tree and flower, they titter with self-pleasure at the dullness it takes bad sex and liquor to shine, but the bucket lives by another code, the bucket has stood still in the weeds for decades, become an elder to the malnourished children who come and kick it like a cheap head-stone, or a relic, or a cup for extinct ogres, and when it rains, the hole in the bucket, so packed with leaves it leaks slowly like the sun, the hole asks the Earth to breathe up through the water, to softly sing, and she does, and for those who have the ears to hear it, her song fills the whole valley, and at dusk the deer poke their heads from the woods, they follow the sound, stepping gingerly but surely, like hearts to hope, like children to promise, and if you saw it, the movement of their lips as they lowered their heads to drink, you might think they were whispering vespers to the bucket, or to the Earth as she sings to them, some low lullaby of praise in deersong like thank you, bucket, for being here, for taking a long time to depart, we count on you to wet our lips when the clouds fail to appear, they don't fill the sky like they used to, the sky bleeds with the barks of dogs and the shouts of men who let their dogs loose upon us for fun, men who wouldn't even know what to do with our bodies if we died, let alone know how to bury us so we won't haunt them, and we will, we will fill them with a dread so subtle it feels like their own failure, but enough of them, we love you, bucket, and we think of you as we lose the dogs in the brush, as we approach you from across the valley, everything coated in thin white dust, and when we settle into our dens at night, we talk of you, as one might talk of a cupped hand, fading slowly, the rest of the body long departed: a rusty bucket, offering water—all that's left of a god.

So Long as There Is Light, There Is Song

Safora, Addie and I sit in a field, at the edge of tree-shade,
where Addie chews an ice-lolly made of frozen sweet potatoes,
cool to the tongue, cool to the grass as it falls from the sides
of her mouth, refreshes the blades, refreshes her throat,

as seeing her refreshed refreshes us. We take a moment
to thank the tree and the sweet potatoes and the soil
for their succor, and we take several moments to admire
the ants while they march in and out of their little tan hills.

Blessed by the mess, we study the grass that keeps
throwing itself like little green-bodied supplicants at the sun.
There's another one here. The one who lives us.
In whose breath we are held. In whose voice we are sung.

Sometimes gently. Sometimes throat-swole
with the rasp of the storm. You could call it continuity.
You could call it the field itself. I like to call it what calls.
And I like to live in her song. For when the birds dry up

and the trees choke and the grass drowns,
when the soil washes away and the oceans burn off
and the bare rock stares back at the bare light,
the Earth will still be here, singing her duet with the sun.

Hunger

I still recall counting pennies,
rolling them to buy cookies
when I should have bought

vegetables and milk,
and it seems those days could
be tomorrow,

hunger gnawing
at the lining of my gut,
the grass in the yard

calling the horses
back into my limbs,
my neck growing

long
with weakness,
my head drooping

until my nose
brushes the blades
and all I can do

is lip the green graces
into my mouth
and nip.

Rascal

The rooster entered the circle of dirt
ceded to my dog on his chain.
All that remained was a few stray feathers.

Later, we fenced the yard and he rushed
the fool boys who barked at him,
knowing he would make them bleed
as he made my father bleed
when he raised his hand against me.

Later still, the fence came down
and he roamed the neighborhood,
fucking and fighting like a lord
until I stood on the porch
and called out to him—

Rascal, Rascal, Rascal—

pausing after each incantation to listen:
at first the faint jingle of his collar,
and then the full force of him
tearing down the middle of the road,

as if daring the cars to come between
him and the boy who called him home.

Glad of the Quiet

The wind cuts across the field
like a scythe
and my mind is blank, has been this way for months,

I don't even *want* to write a poem—
it hurts
but I like the hurt: at last

I stand among my friends
and feel no desire
to snip the shadows from their feet.

Day of My Death

The ghosts we carry sweep ahead of and behind us,
the flapping of wings we've forgotten how to feel—
each death a feather, a shiver, a swallow. We keep it down.

I talk to the air, might be mad, but since when is talking
to someone crazy? I have a whole lifetime's worth of people—
friends, lovers, family, foes—who live inside me.

People I never spoke to. People I never want to speak to again.
I'd kick some out if I could, but the landlord has no address,
and the terms of the lease stretch out further than I can trail,

all the way down to where the river revels in its return
to the ocean, and the body bleeds heat like a sun
close to the end of its fuel. I imagine that day, gusty,

sharkfins visible from the shore, a seagull circling
something dark and tasty in the water, a violent storm
moving in, the worms rejoicing, the crow flying low

and cropping the hair on Addie's head, who lifts
her nose to test the air then lowers it, the scent of her life
a little emptier than the last time she checked.

Death on the Iron Escape

Today the feathers fell like snow
from the fire escape two floors above.
The season was right, the weather,
the chill chewing my blood,
numbing my skin, my muscles
shaking as if an all-pervasive
meth dealer fed me the icy air.

But the falling was all wrong.
At first one feather, and then another,
and then clumps of them filled
my window while, two stories above,
the hawk tore the head from the neck
and the heart from the chest
and gave the pigeon
a bigger pair of wings to fly.

He left the carcass for the neighbor
in apartment 67 to gnaw.
I wish she were the one gone to rot.
I wish we were the ones gone to rot.
What the hell is wrong with me?
What kind of human wants
to see the backside of humankind?
What kind of human doesn't?

My Favorite Sweater

The moths have come and gone again another season.
Left portals in my coats and sweaters. I hope they
had a good meal, that the relics of sweat didn't cause them

too much indigestion. They even supped on my favorite,
a third-hand green the color of pine, thick as a blanket,
the goats right up against me as the cold tries to stick

its hand into my chest. I hope they ate well enough
to bear another generation without the hunger
and suffering too many have known. Another hand

would hunt them down and smack the light
from their lamps, but today, as the Christmas sun
makes its five-minute visit through my north window,

where the cut flowers gave up their color in a month
I can't recall—today, I wish the moths no ill.
I finger the holes they made in their service to hunger

and say to myself *it's all down to pattern, a shifting
pattern*, a thread of wool raveling into a thread of moth,
the moth's wings the stitchwork of the hand that knits us all,

the hand itself a stich along a seam my mind unravels
attempting to recall. So I ponder the sweater, its genesis,
its journey, the unseen influence of the bodies that bore it

unto the spinner's loom, and the bodies that bought it and wore it
before me. And I thank the goats and I thank the grass and I thank
the knitter whose brow furrowed over the intelligent design,

roomy in the shoulders, where my joints tend to complain.
And I thank the moths for their generosity, leaving plenty
of the forest-green cashmere to keep me warm.

I thank until I run out of things to thank, and the candle
burns low, and the whiskey disappears, and the night
calls me down. I take off the sweater and leave it,

hanging, uncovered in the closet, quietly inviting
the moths to come, to settle, to unhinge their mouths
and let the Earth knit their soft bodies again.

Impatience

Come in, moth—
I have a candle just for you.

My Favorite Time of Day Is
When the Light Begins to Dim

I have two suns, one on either side
of my nose. They light the way.
They deceive me. They apply the thin
film of desire to the world as it exists
and show me the world as I wish to see it.
I have tried to break them of the habit,
but it's like cleaning windows:
by the time you're done they're already
filling up with impurities, distractions,
the warp of one's will distorting the view.
I mean I lie to myself
to take the sting out of hours.
I put the stingers in a pile.
When it's about the size of an impossible
cherry, I eat all the honesty
at once. So bitter you can imagine why
the universe wanted one
of its constituents to be honey.

I hold a gallon of it up to the light
and could spend hours lost in the labyrinth
of its imperfections, which don't exist.
My ophthalmologist, in his southern
drawl, calls me honey, orders
unnecessary tests to make money,
his honesty about as discernable

as the morning's hint of evening's
heat. He says the suns on either side
of my nose may be dimming before
their time. My trusty lanterns, the bastard.
But he might know of what he speaks.
The way his mind drifts, his speech slows,
and the words fall apart in his mouth,
I think he has dimmed before his time.
Which is a terrible thing to say,
terrible the way truth is a weapon:
one we must use or die.

On Hurricanes

I'm a Florida boy, beachtown born, so listen closely.
You know it's coming when the insects hush,
when the sky agitates and the door slams shut,
the talons of the wind having snatched it from my fingers.

Then the squall seems to have an argument with itself,
the trees catching the worst of it, the branches slapped left,
right, up, down. Cue the rain, vengeful in her nourishment,
gravity all at once gutting the belly of every cloud.

Meanwhile, under the eaves, two fingers pinch out
each flicker of birdsong, toss their nests to the floor.
The snakes hiss in approval. The alligators
slap their tails as they climb the swollen banks.

The ocean batters its mind against the shore
and the fish grow afraid in their element.
The cats claw each other for the closet's corner.
Addie runs from the whip of thunder.

I run with her, kneel beside her, promise I will
let no harm befall her, and though I cannot keep
that promise, I will put my body between her
and the flying glass if that's what it takes.

Then the rain turns violent, pounded by some invisible
hammer, nailing everything to the Earth. The wind, too:
strips the trees of their branches, the ground of its trees,
plucks the chimney like a red leaf from the roof.

The walls shake, the ceiling cracks, the windows shatter,
the glass carves my face, and blood flies. The storm
tosses me like a ragdoll against the wall
and I lose sight of Addie, then the sight of myself.

The rough hands of the universe smash my cells
together like pots, like fusion, like retribution—
bang, bang, bang—the roar of it so loud
I can hear the lion's mouth around my head.

We Carry More than We Can Tell

for Nuala Ní Dhomhnaill

Some days, my hands tell me what they've done.
They speak quietly. They show me eleven scars
and remind me that I drove a car, blacked out.

The left lifts his pinky, or what's left of it,
and I wince again at the time
I tried to cut the bread and slipped.

He healed himself and learned to live
a little lighter on the wrist.
The right, well burned, the cooking hand,

pinches turmeric and saffron from their pots,
but ask him for a measurement
and he'll lift his empty palm and scoff.

Some nights, when I watch the stars,
on television or in the sky, I can feel them
under the covers, holding each other like lovers—

I sneak a peek but it's too tender,
so I look away, embarrassed to watch.
But don't let them fool you.

They're brawlers. They're killers.
I've seen them take a knife to a fish
and gut it in thirty seconds flat.

I'm grateful but it scares me.
Where'd they get the knack?
They learn quicker, master better

than anything else I have.
Should I trust them when my lover
prefers them in the sack?

Am I cruel when I remember the blizzard and they shiver,
pale as two forget-me-nots in my lap?
Should I offer them comfort when the bed is empty,

when the sheets are cold,
when their knuckles crackle with arthritis
and even their old magic won't bring her back?

Lamb's Lung: Addie's Favorite Treat

Breath of lamb in my pocket
I break its days into thumb-sized pieces,

press the brown communion
onto Addie's pink tongue.

Each treat is a pick-me-up
but ten lungs isn't enough to sate her—

she'd eat until she spewed
and eat again.

I'm making this up
out of what I know of the truth,

how it hurts,
how desire leads us astray,

how this treat was once a lamb
in love with its pasture,

how I want the pleasure in Addie's eyes
as she eats

and asks for another
to be enough,

but nothing is.

Read Slowly

Because every day we turn a page,
and a little less
of our story awaits us.

Hannah

Every morning, the grass squeaks under my daughter's wet feet and she attends the temple of crow. A black spot against the blue sky clutching his wire throne. Obsidian risen from lava to wing, where the light iridesces like the shine on a pearl. Hannah greets him *good morning* and tosses her wish for the day into his well. She says he studies her while the wish enters his eye and whistles down the flutes of his bones. I ask her where it goes and she says: *towards a special place the crow and I share.* When I ask her where that is, she says *I can't tell you*, and when I her ask why not, she says *because I don't know how, and if I did, the crow would curse me.* I think it's the place where fledgling wishes are pushed from the nest into water. If they guzzle the whole ocean, they survive. If they drink once and wipe their mouths, they disappear. A wish's truth is passion or perish. And for Hannah to tell me of their special place would be to break the spell. She tells me anyways, says that when a wish reaches the crow's heart, he looks away from her and caws. He tests the wish, and if it survives him, he gives it back to her, and it circles in her, like the wind unwrapping the stones from a well. She says she waits for the wish to reveal its destiny—yes or no—and when it's a good one, when it's about to come true, the wish asks her if she's ready enter its world. Hannah is *my* wish, my good one, and I hope she will come true any day now.

So Tired Any Rest Is Grace

When the cancer
bloomed like an angry
flower in her liver

she said *thank you, I'm so tired,*
I've been wondering
when you would arrive.

Help me out of these clothes,
would you, then
help me out of these bones.

Another Poet Supernovas into the Dark

for Mardah Chami, in memoriam

I crumple my hat and dry tears. It smells like the dust
of all the poems that tried to cross my lips and died.
That won't do, just now. A good woman, a poet,
a friend, has supernova'd into the dark: left children,
a husband, hundreds like me: sunk and wanting
one more minute before they lower her into the ground.

We'll get it, not the minute we want, but the minutes
we had, fleeing us, teasing us, fireflies mapping
the course of the past we wish we could hold but can't.
We'll follow them, hunt them, dowsing for a door
to the secret field where our nights, always too few
and too hurried, could continue: uninterrupted.

Could never end: so that even when we wake up
and face the disintegration of our own faces,
and the faces of everyone we know, we'll still be there,
under the stars, our bodies quietly burning, sharing a word
and a laugh, as if we had spent our whole lives preparing
ourselves as gifts for one another, as indeed we have.

Picking Myself Up Off the Floor

The sun walks away from me
and the dark says hello again

and I spin through my memories
like arguments against

my continued existence
until the cacophony is deafening

so I close my eyes, I plug my ears
and I scream until the dark hums

and my head clears and the frogs pause
and the man in the moon

looks up from his book
to consider my soliloquy

and all the things about to happen
line up like urges in my hands.

A Walk in the Woods

Addie has a little rush in her step as we enter the woods.
She isn't alone. Fall feels like someone has stuck his hand
in and snipped out my soul, I mean the hand has come out
wearing the most exquisite glove the weather has to offer
and is waving everywhere at me in godcolors and golds.

But there's something missing: the chill within:
the soul's absence calling it back. I'm not sure it should listen,
at least not yet. I'm trying to unlearn the rhythms of the city.
Maybe I can't, but already the woods feel like home.
Humans were never a species I was given to understand.

My kind have rough barks, trunks and a desire to hold steady,
which may be a function of how poorly my legs work. Then again,
does any species understand itself? That's a question for the ether,
not the ear. In the forest the walls of my mind come down
and thoughts stumble out of their tortured apartments to think.

The world *is* spacious, after all. And my arboreal friends
are busy perfecting the seven-thousand kinds of quiet.
It's conversational, not shushes but whispers that spill from branch
to branch the secrets of the Earth. These secrets: to know them
is to live them, they spend the way a conductor moves his hand.

And the trees are full of conductors. Every time I look up
into a canopy, I see a mind at work. Whose, though?
Did the trees conjure birdsong? Or did the birds sing the trees
up and around them? Or did they meet in the middle,
treesong trilling an outlet in feathered throats?

At some point the birds lift up in unison and flock out of sight.
The leaves flap and fall like waves upon the water.
The estuary of the mind gives way to the amniotic ocean
it inhabits

     and the sensation

          is no longer

               one of walking:

     it's one of being walked.

About the Author

Ricky Ray is a disabled poet, critic, essayist and the founding editor of *Rascal: A Journal of Ecology, Literature and Art*. He is the author of the full-length collection, *Fealty* (Diode Editions, 2019), and two chapbooks: *Quiet, Grit, Glory* (Broken Sleep Books, 2020), and *The Sound of the Earth Singing to Herself* (Fly on the Wall Press, 2020). His awards include the Cormac McCarthy Prize, the Ron McFarland Poetry Prize, and a Liam Rector fellowship. His work appears widely in periodicals and anthologies, including *The American Scholar, Verse Daily, Diode Poetry Journal* and *The Moth*. He was educated at Columbia University and the Bennington Writing Seminars, and lives on the outskirts of the Hudson Valley, where he can be found hobbling in the old green hills with his old brown dog, Addie.

About Fly on the Wall Press

A publisher with a conscience.
Publishing high quality anthologies on pressing issues,
chapbooks and poetry products, from exceptional poets around
the globe. Founded in 2018 by founding editor, Isabelle Kenyon.

Other publications in order of publication:
Please Hear What I'm Not Saying (Anthology, profits to Mind.)
Persona Non Grata (Anthology, profits to Shelter and Crisis Aid
UK.)
Bad Mommy / Stay Mommy by Elisabeth Horan
The Woman With An Owl Tattoo by Anne Walsh Donnelly
the sea refuses no river by Bethany Rivers
White Light White Peak by Simon Corble
Second Life by Karl Tearney
The Dogs of Humanity by Colin Dardis
Planet in Peril (Anthology, profits to WWF and The Climate
Coalition.)
Small Press Publishing: The Dos and Don'ts by Isabelle Kenyon
Alcoholic Betty by Elisabeth Horan
Awakening by Sam Love
Grenade Genie by Tom McColl
House of Weeds by Amy Kean and Jack Wallington
No Home In This World by Kevin Crowe
The Goddess of Macau by Graeme Hall
How To Make Curry Goat by Louise McStravick
The Prettyboys of Gangster Town by Martin Grey

Social Media:
@fly_press (Twitter) @flyonthewall_poetry (Instagram)
@flyonthewallpoetry (Facebook)
www.flyonthewallpoetry.co.uk

9 781913 211318